19.97

WA

D1539474

DATE DUE Y94

MAR 2 4 1995		
DEC 2 7 1995		
JUL 8 1996		

Exploring Music

Brass

Alyn Shipton

RSVP

RAINTREE
STECK-VAUGHN
P U B L I S H E R S
The Steck-Vaughn Company

Austin, Texas

Titles in the Series
Brass
Keyboards and Electronic Music
Percussion
Singing
Strings
Woodwinds

Edited by Pauline Tait
Picture research by Suzanne Williams
Designed by Julian Holland
Illustrator: Terry Hadler
Electronic Production: Scott Melcer

Picture acknowledgments
Raintree Steck-Vaughn Publishers would like to thank Edgarley Hall School music department, especially Mr. Brian Armfield, for assistance with commissioned photography; and David Titchener for supplying the photographs.

The author and publishers wish to thank the following photographic sources: Courtesy of Amon Ra Records: p8 (top), p9 (bottom); The Bate Collection of Historical Instruments, Faculty of Music, University of Oxford: p22; Courtesy of The Black Dyke Mills Band: p26/Pippin Photography; The Bridgeman Art Library, Denis van Alsloot (1570-c. 1626) *Detail from a Procession*, Private Collection: p14 (top), Conservatoire National Supérieur de Musique, Paris: p23 (top); Nationalmuseet, Copenhagen: p21 (right)/Kit Weiss; C.M. Dixon: p5 (bottom), p21 (left); E.T. Archive: p5 (top); Gebrüder Alexander Mainz: p28; The Hutchison Library: p20, p27 (bottom), p29 (bottom right); The Image Bank: p6/Alvis Upitis; The London Serpent-Trio, courtesy of Prelude: p9 (top); Performing Arts Library/Clive Barda: p17, p23 (bottom); Redferns: title page/Odile Noel, p11 (top), p12, p13, p16, p18/Odile Noel; Courtesy of Sotheby's, London: p8 (bottom); Zefa: p15, p19, p29 (top), p29 (bottom left).

Cover credits
(trombones & tuba) © Odile Noel/Redferns;
(marching band) © Zefa.

Library of Congress Cataloging-in-Publication Data

Shipton, Alyn.
    Brass / Alyn Shipton.
       p.   cm. — (Exploring music)
    Includes index.
    Summary: Text and pictures introduce the brass family of instruments, such as trumpets, trombones, tubas, and their relatives.
    ISBN 0-8114-2317-4
    1. Brass instruments — Juvenile literature.   1. Brass instruments.]
  I. Title.   II. Series: Shipton, Alyn. Exploring music.
ML933.S52   1994
788.9' 19—dc20
                                        93-2895
                                           CIP
                                       MN AC

Printed and bound in the United States
1 2 3 4 5 6 7 8 9 0 VHP 99 98 97 96 95 94 93

Contents

♪ What Is a Brass Instrument?

All brass instruments work in the same way. They are each made from a metal tube. At one end is a **mouthpiece**, and at the other is a flared **bell**. The player rests the cup-shaped mouthpiece over his or her mouth. The lips "buzz" into the cup of the mouthpiece as the player breathes out. This sets up vibrations in the tube, producing the sound. The technical name for a brass mouthpiece is a **lip reed**.

Played on its own, the mouthpiece makes a strange chirpy sound. Skilled players use it for trick effects, sometimes attaching it to a teapot or a piece of hose. The notes can be made higher by tightening the lips, and lower by loosening them. Blowing hard makes them louder, but has no effect on pitch. To start a note, the player quickly pulls back the tongue from behind the front teeth — sort of like spitting out a grape seed or a cherry pit.

How Do Notes Change?

Two things affect the note a brass instrument plays. The first is the speed at which the player's lips vibrate against the mouthpiece. The second is the length of the tube.

On the next page, we can see how the length of tubing differs in the various members of the brass family. But what happens when the player changes the frequency of the vibrations in the tube?

horn

flugelhorn

tuba

Brass instrument mouthpieces

Sound

When any object is made to vibrate, it produces a sound. Our ears can detect the sound because the vibration pushes or pulls the air close to it, forming sound waves. These waves carry the sound through the air just as waves travel over water.

Big, loud sounds, like a ship's horn, create huge sound waves that can be heard for miles. Tiny sounds, like the delicate footsteps of a cat, create such small sound waves that they are hard to hear, even if you are nearby.

Our ears tell sounds from one another by identifying three things about each one:

volume: how loud it is;

pitch: how high or low it is; and

tone: the type or quality of the sound

Because no two things vibrate in quite the same way, the pattern of sound waves they produce is different. This means that even if two musical instruments play a note of the same volume and pitch, they will sound different from one another.

THE HARMONIC SERIES

A player can raise the pitch of a sound, using the mouthpiece, by tightening the lips. This is because tight lips vibrate faster than if they remain loose and floppy.

Inside the tube of a brass instrument, the **air column** itself vibrates in different ways. As well as vibrating along the whole length of the tube, the air can also vibrate in fractions (small regular sections) of the tube's length.

The diagram on this page shows that as the air in the tube vibrates more quickly, more notes can be made. The note produced when air vibrates along the whole tube is the lowest note, called the **fundamental**. The other notes, made when air vibrates in fractions of the tube, are called harmonics. You will see that if the bottom note made by the tube is B♭ (B flat), the faster vibrations produce a series of notes that join into a B♭ **chord**. The series of notes is called the **harmonic series**.

A British bugler of the 1800s from the 20th Hussars regiment

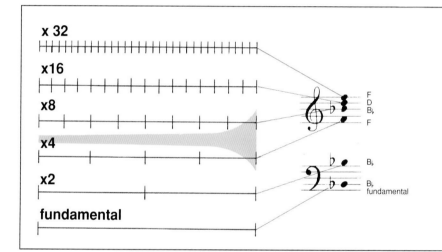

The Harmonic Series
This shows the series of notes in the B♭ chord, made as the air vibrates in fractions of the tube. To make top F the air is vibrating 32 times faster than bottom B♭, the fundamental.

SIMPLE BRASS INSTRUMENTS

Some brass instruments have tubes of fixed length, so that the only way they can change their notes is through the harmonic series. Among them is the military bugle. When the notes in the diagram are played on the piano, you will find they are the familiar notes of the bugle call. Other simple brass instruments include the hunting horn, the alphorn, and the post horn.

The biggest lip-reed instrument is the Swiss alpenhorn, made of wood, not brass. This one is being played in front of the Matterhorn, a mountain in Switzerland.

Valves and Slides

If the only notes we could get out of brass instruments were those of the bugle call, they would be very dull indeed. If, however, you could alter the length of the tube so that the bottom note, or fundamental, changed, then you could get a new bugle call with a different harmonic series from the same instrument. Instrument builders have solved the problem in two ways, to make a set of bugle calls that allows the player to produce all the normal notes of the scale.

The two main ways to change the length of the tube are by using the **valves** or a **slide**.

The trombone (left) changes its notes with a slide. The trumpeter (right) uses his right hand to operate the instrument's valves.

VALVES

The valve is a kind of switch that controls an extra length of tubing. With the valve open, the extra tubing is added to the air column of the instrument. With the valve closed, this extra tubing is shut off. Most brass instruments have three valves, operated by the first three fingers of the right hand. A set of different lengths of tube can be made by pressing down the valves one at a time or together.

Each valve can be adjusted to allow the player to make sure the extra length of tubing it controls is exactly right to produce new notes in tune with the fundamental. These are called **tuning slides.**

Different valves
(arrows show direction of air)

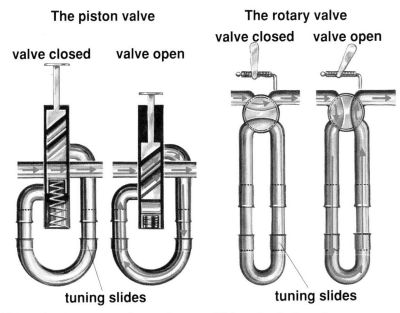

The piston valve

valve closed   valve open

The rotary valve

valve closed   valve open

tuning slides

tuning slides

This valve is commonly used on American, English, and French brass instruments.

This valve is found on many modern horns and tubas made in Germany.

THE SLIDE

The other method used to change the length of a brass instrument's tube, or air column, is the slide. At one time, many instruments, including the sackbut and the slide trumpet, used this method. Today, only the trombone has a slide. It works very simply. One length of tube slides outside another, varying the overall length. You can see from the diagram that, by stopping the slide in regular positions, the player can obtain seven different harmonic series. By moving the slide between positions all the notes on the scale can be found using the harmonic series based on each of the seven fundamental notes.

The harmonic series of the tenor trombone

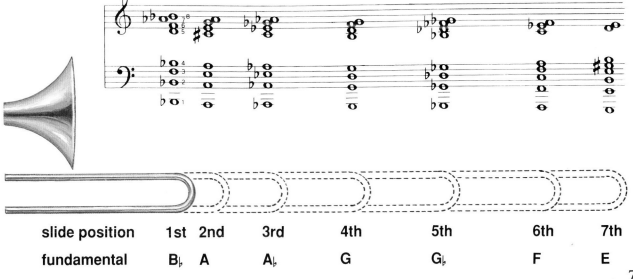

slide position	1st	2nd	3rd	4th	5th	6th	7th
fundamental	B♭	A	A♭	G	G♭	F	E

♪ Early Brass Instruments

Before instrument makers and inventors settled on valves and slides as the best way of changing the notes made by brass instruments, they tried out other ideas. The simplest was to make holes in the sound tube, like those in a woodwind instrument, and to combine this with a lip-reed mouthpiece.

One of the earliest instruments built like this, in the 12th century, was the cornett. The body of the cornett was made of wood, and instead of being round, the **profile** was sharply angled, somewhat like a pencil.

The longer an early cornett was, the lower the notes it played. If it got too big, the finger holes became too far apart for the player's hand to cover them easily. The answer was to bend the tube, and this led to a very unusual instrument called the serpent. A metal tube, with the trumpetlike mouthpiece at the top, leads to the long snakelike body of the serpent, which is sometimes covered in black leather. The finger holes are cut into the two sections of the body that cross horizontally in front of the player.

Another kind of cornett was the Russian bassoon. It was more or less the same to listen to, or to play, as a serpent, but the tube was bent double instead of curved, and it looked more like a bassoon. Russian bassoons often have elaborate bells made to look like animal or dragon heads. These are made of brass and are painted bright colors, or sometimes a reddish brown.

The early cornett had a mouthpiece like a brass instrument, but finger holes like those of a recorder changed the notes.

This serpent, made in 1825, has a black leather body kept in shape by metal supports. Two keys operate notes that would be out of reach of the player's fingers. The mouthpiece is carved from ivory.

The London Serpent Trio demonstrates the unusual method of playing this instrument, in a very unusual setting!

KEYED BRASS INSTRUMENTS

Another attempt to produce a full range of notes from brass instruments, without using valves or slides, dates from about 1810. The inventor Joseph Halliday fitted a bugle with **keys**. This allowed the bugler to change the harmonic series by operating the keys in turn to open pads that changed the length of the air column. Composers seized on the invention, and parts were written for the keyed bugle by many 19th-century composers, including Meyerbeer and Rossini.

In 1821, a **bass** version of the keyed bugle was invented, called the ophicleide. It was hard to play in tune and disappeared with the invention of the tuba.

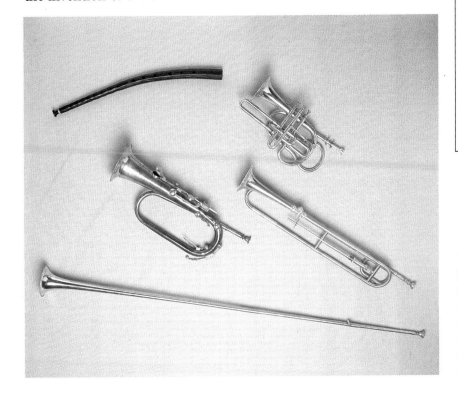

Listening Guide
The cornett was used as a solo instrument to play exciting display music. It was no longer popular by the 17th century, but groups like the Early Music Consort have rediscovered and recorded pieces for it, including pieces by the 16th-century musician Giovanni Gabrieli of Venice.

Serpents were often used in church music. Some English and French churches used to have bands to accompany their services. Serpents were often included in these bands, as well as in some military groups. Twentieth-century composers (including Peter Maxwell Davies) have written for it, and the London Serpent Trio has made records of original music for this unusual instrument.

This group of early brass instruments includes an early cornett (top left), a cornet (top right—see p. 12), a keyed bugle (center left), and a posthorn (bottom). The other instrument is an early kind of trumpet with a slide instead of valves.

𝄞 The Trumpet

The first trumpets had no valves and were called "natural trumpets." These were like long thin bugles, and the player had to be skilled in finding the right notes from the very high section of the harmonic series. Today, the B♭ (B flat) instrument with three valves, shown in the diagram on this page, is the most common form of trumpet. The diagram shows all its different components, including the springs that close the valves when the player lifts the fingers. This kind of trumpet was first made in 1826.

The trumpet has such a clear, brilliant tone partly because its tube is the same thickness from near the mouthpiece all the way down to a few inches before it flares out into the bell.

There are other kinds of trumpets, and like the B♭ instrument, they are named after the fundamental note they play with none of the valves in use. The D trumpet is one-third (two tones) higher than the B♭ trumpet, and is used for high parts. Higher still is the piccolo trumpet, a whole **octave** above the ordinary B♭ instrument. The diagram shows the different sizes of these trumpets, and the differences in their shapes.

Some trumpets are designed for special ceremonial use, and the sound tube extends straight out in front of the valves. A flag or standard can be hung out from the long bell, like the ones used by trumpeters in the inauguration of President Bill Clinton. These are also used in other ceremonial events.

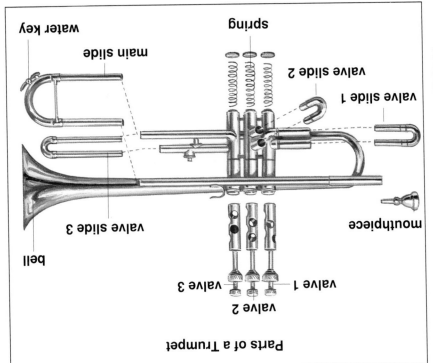

Parts of a Trumpet

water key
main slide
spring
valve slide 2
valve slide 1
valve slide 3
bell
mouthpiece
valve 3
valve 1
valve 2

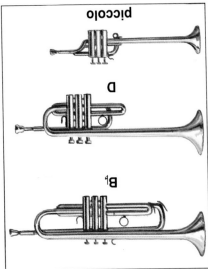

piccolo
D
B♭

Louis Armstrong

CHANGING THE TONE OF THE TRUMPET

The normal sound a trumpet makes is called its "open" tone. Players can change the quality of a trumpet's sound by partly blocking or covering the bell of the instrument with a **mute**. The mute alters the sound waves made by the trumpet. The pitch of the note will be the same, because the same length of air column is vibrating, but the volume and tone will change.

Mutes are made of metal or plastic and come in a variety of shapes and sizes to produce different effects. Jazz trumpet and trombone players frequently use mutes.

Listening Guide

Composers in the 1600s and 1700s wrote for natural trumpets, with no valves. Players now use modern instruments for pieces by J.S. Bach (his Brandenburg Concerto No. 2) and G.F. Handel ("The trumpet shall sound" from *Messiah*). There are many trumpet concertos. Very famous ones by Handel and Hummel have been recorded by Maurice André and Wynton Marsalis.

The trumpet has also been very important in jazz. New Orleans players like Louis Armstrong played the melody in early jazz records like "West End Blues." Later, Dizzy Gillespie, Miles Davis, and Maynard Ferguson made jazz records to show off their technique, tone, and range. Listen to Gillespie's "Night in Tunisia" or "Groovin' High," Davis's "Kind of Blue," and Ferguson's high notes in his "Big Bop Nouveau."

Trumpet Playing

If you want to learn the trumpet, you'll start with the ordinary B♭ instrument. Usually you'll need to wait until you've got all your permanent teeth, since the position of the trumpet against your lips and teeth is important. Progress will be slow at first, since it is hard to get the upper notes in the harmonic series until your mouth muscles have developed. The technical name for this is your **embouchure,** but most brass players say you need to develop your "lip."

Even if you start on a borrowed instrument, you'll quickly want one of your own. Second-hand trumpets are not a good idea, as sticking valves and weak springs can make them hard to play. Buying a new trumpet can be expensive, but it is the best way of ensuring that everything works properly.

♪ Relatives of the Trumpet

THE CORNET

The B♭ cornet is very similar to the trumpet. It has a tube that flares more gradually toward the bell, unlike the parallel tube of the trumpet. It is also a different shape, as you can see in the picture.

The cornet has a softer, less brilliant tone than the trumpet, and it is considered easier to play. It has always played the main melody in brass bands.

Ruby Braff playing the cornet

Cornet Playing

Because the design of the cornet is so much like the trumpet, it is very similar to play, so learning both instruments is almost the same. Many players move easily from one instrument to the other. If you want to play in a brass or silver band, then the cornet is the instrument to learn. Its larger mouthpiece and softer tone make it ideal for the mellow sound of a brass band. It lacks the "heraldic" sound of the trumpet, so it is not often used in orchestral music, nor is it as popular for jazz as the trumpet.

THE FLUGELHORN

The flugelhorn is only a distant relation of the trumpet, but it is usually pitched in B♭ and is similar to play. It looks like a bugle with three trumpet valves stuck on the side, and that is more or less what it is. The flugelhorn has a deep soft tone, and some classical composers have written special solo passages for it. Like the cornet, the flugelhorn is found in most brass bands.

Listening Guide

To hear brass bands using cornets and flugelhorns, listen to records by the Brighouse and Rastrick Brass Band.

In jazz there are records by many cornetists from the 1920s, including the young Louis Armstrong on "Cornet Chop Suey," "Potato Head Blues," and "West End Blues."

The flugelhorn appears in Vaughan Williams's Symphony No. 9 and has also been played by jazz musicians like Shorty Rogers, Miles Davis, Freddie Hubbard, Chuck Mangione, and Ian Carr.

This photograph shows how much bigger the flugelhorn is than the trumpet or cornet. You can see how the valves fit on this bugle-shaped instrument being played by Freddie Hubbard.

The Trombone

The first trombones date from the late 1400s. They were called sackbuts and were played in bands at royal festivals and weddings. In a painting from the 1490s on a church wall in Italy, one of a group of flying angels is shown playing the sackbut.

The oldest trombone in the world was made in Nuremburg in 1551, and is preserved in the museum there. It has a rather small bell that doesn't flare out as far as does the bell on a modern instrument. Like all trombones, it was designed to be taken apart when it was not being used. The sliding section and the bell are made to lock into one another for playing, but they come apart and pack alongside one another. This means that the long, thin instrument can be carried easily.

Trombones were built in many different sizes. The smallest is a version of the trumpet with a slide instead of valves. It is very difficult to play in tune and is almost never used, though in the 1920s it was popular as a novelty instrument. Early pictures of the jazz player Louis Armstrong show him posing with a slide trumpet, but he never played the instrument seriously. Today, the three common sizes for the trombone are **alto, tenor,** and **bass.** The instrument most of us recognize is the tenor, which is the most popular.

The nearer musician in this 16th-century Flemish picture is playing a sackbut.

tenor trombone

bass trombone

This diagram shows the difference in size between the tenor and bass trombones. The bass has a larger bell and extra tubing.

THE ALTO TROMBONE

The small alto instrument is less common, and players tend to keep it for long high notes that need to be played softly. Benjamin Britten wrote a special part for the alto trombone in *The Burning Fiery Furnace*.

THE TENOR TROMBONE

In brass bands and orchestras, the trombone **section** is mainly made up of tenor trombones. In the picture of the parade below, you can see some of the trombones marching at the front. This is so that their long slides don't hit anyone in front of them as they march along!

THE BASS TROMBONE

The bass trombone is the biggest of the family. It has a much larger flared bell than the tenor. This makes it easy to spot the bass trombonist in the brass section of an orchestra. Most bass trombonists play an instrument with extra tubing placed in the bell section of the instrument, over the player's shoulder. By operating a valve that opens or shuts this extra tube, the player can make the instrument work like a tenor trombone (with the tube shut) or a bass (with the tube open).

The Valve Trombone

In the 19th century, inventors designed and built trombones that had valves instead of a slide. In many ways, these were like huge trumpets, and were slightly shorter than the normal trombone with its slide "closed." For some kinds of music, valve trombones became very popular. Mounted military bands discovered that it is almost impossible to use both hands to play the slide trombone while staying balanced on horseback. So they were very pleased with valve instruments. Brass bands, especially in continental Europe, liked the valve trombone, and today it is still used in many parts of the world.

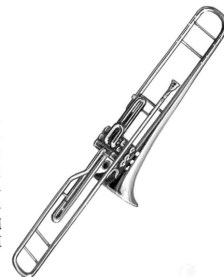

The valve trombone is almost always a tenor instrument. This picture shows how the instrument differs from the slide trombone.

Trombone Playing

When a beginner takes up the trombone, it can seem an impossible instrument to play well. Finding the correct positions for the slide is hard at first, and so is controlling the lips to produce the different notes in the harmonic series.

There are few brass instruments that can produce so many effects. The slide allows the players to adjust pitch very finely. Dr. William Stone, a 19th-century writer, said "trombone-playing, when thoroughly learned, more nearly approaches that of good voice production than any other instrument."

Players have rediscovered the skill of smooth **legato** playing that Dr. Stone admired. In contrast, some musicians have developed great speed on the trombone, while others have discovered a way of playing several notes at the same time called **multiphonics**. The German trombonist Alfred Mangelsdorff is a specialist in unusual ways of playing the trombone.

Listening Guide

The trombone appears in orchestral music by many composers, including Mozart, Brahms, Strauss, and Wagner. Listen for the trombone in the "Tuba Mirum" section of Mozart's *Requiem.* Prokofiev used the instrument in his suite *Lieutenant Kije*.

In jazz, the slurs and slides of the trombone were used by Kid Dry for his "Dry's Creole Trombone," while the high, pure, singing quality of the instrument was captured by Tommy Dorsey in his theme song "I'm Getting Sentimental over You." Other jazz musicians like J.J. Johnson and Frank Rosolino use the trombone slide to play dazzling fast passages. Some rock bands have brass "sections," with trombones and trumpets. Elvis Costello has used brass instruments with his touring groups.

You can see the trombones over the shoulder of the tuba player. The trombones are at the back of the orchestra's brass section, and here they are in front of a chorus.

The Tuba

The tuba is a very much younger instrument than the trombone. It was invented in 1835 by the bandmaster Wilhelm Wieprecht to replace the unwieldy and inaccurate ophicleide as the bass member of the brass family.

In the symphony orchestra, you will see the tuba player sitting alongside the trombone section. The instrument is held on the player's lap and supported by the left hand. The right hand operates the valves. Most orchestral tubas have four valves (including the "double C" instrument and the huge contrabass E♭ instrument used in Britain).

The bell of the tuba is widely flared, and sometimes you will see a player using a mute that fits into it. Unlike the small mutes used to alter the sound of the trumpet, a tuba mute is big — it looks sort of like a galvanized bucket! The mute muffles the sound of the instrument. When it is played by itself, the tuba has a smooth, mellow sound. The cup-shaped mouthpiece, like almost everything else about the instrument, is large. A skilled player can get a vast range of notes out of the tuba, from the very deep fundamental notes of the harmonic series to higher notes well into the upper range of the trombone or French horn.

The picture of the tuba (above) shows the basic instrument with three valves. When a fourth valve is fitted, it is often played by the left hand. Look closely at the orchestral player in the photograph on the right, and you will just see his left hand working this extra valve.

Tuba Playing

To play the tuba, as with learning the double bass in the string family, you have to be big enough to hold and, in this case, blow into the instrument properly before you can start to learn it. If you join an orchestra or brass band, you will find many composers have written simple "oompah" parts, and you can quickly take part. If you want to play in a marching or military band, you might want to play one of the relatives of the tuba shown on the next page.

Otherwise you will need a sling that goes around your neck and hooks onto a ring on the tuba to support it while you're on the move. The mouthpiece is big and deep, and you need great lip control to play in tune (especially the higher notes). You will be able to produce a wide range of notes fairly easily, because the lips remain fairly slack inside the "cup" of the mouthpiece.

Listening Guide

Composers like Berlioz and Wagner wrote for orchestral brass sections with several tubas, including short solo passages. Vaughan Williams wrote a concerto for the tuba, and Hindemith composed a solo sonata for it. In the first jazz bands the tuba was used instead of the double bass, by players like John Kirby and Billy Taylor.

Unusual Tubas

THE HELICON

The orchestral tuba has its sound pipe coiled up so that the instrument sits on the player's lap. In 19th-century Europe, inventors tried curling the tubing in a different way, so that it formed a broad loop, running over the player's shoulder. This new instrument was called the helicon, and it became popular in marching bands because it was much easier to carry than the normal tuba. The helicon had quite a narrow bell, which pointed into the air above the player.

THE SOUSAPHONE

The most famous band director and composer of band music in the U.S. in the 1890s was John Philip Sousa. He modified the helicon, in 1898, to make it more suitable for his marching and concert bands. He made the bell larger and swiveled it around, so that it pointed forward. The valves are placed across the player's front and are operated by the right hand. Sousa realized that the shape of his new instrument made it hard to carry when it was not being used. He made the bell detachable, so that for carrying it packs neatly inside the loop of the main tubing. Today, to save weight, the bell is often made of fiberglass, but original sousaphones were very heavy and could get caught by gusts of wind!

The unmistakable shape of four sousaphones being played in a South American parade

Part of a carved column that shows three Roman musicians playing the *cornu*

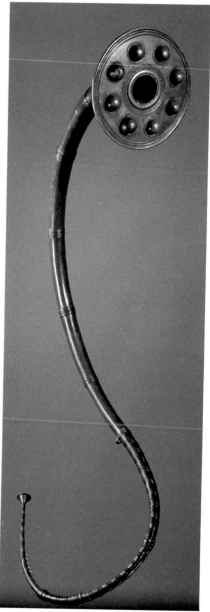

NOT SUCH A NEW IDEA...

The 19th-century band directors who invented the helicon and the sousaphone might have been surprised to find out that some of the ideas had been tried out hundreds of years earlier! In ancient Rome, players used an instrument that looked sort of like the sousaphone. It was called the *cornu* and had a simple bronze tube like a bugle, bent into a kind of G-shape. The bell pointed forward over the player's shoulder, and a wooden support fitted across to act as a grip, in exactly the place the more modern instruments have their valves. Carvings of Roman processions show bands playing these instruments.

Even earlier, in the Bronze Age, musicians in what are now parts of Sweden and Denmark played the *lur*. Archaeologists have found many examples of the *lur* in peat bogs. They have been well preserved by the peat and show us how these ancient instruments looked. The tubing is about ten feet long and ends in a beautifully decorated disk in place of the modern bell. Often, these instruments have been found in pairs, which suggests they were played together. The remains have been found of rattles and bells that hung from the sound pipe and added to the loud and raucous sound of the *lur*. The name *lur* has survived to describe a wooden trumpet used until recently by Scandinavian shepherds.

A well-preserved Danish example of the *lur*

The French Horn

Up to six French horns belong to the brass section of the orchestra. The modern instrument has **rotary valves** that are worked by the player's left hand. The instrument is supported by the right hand, which is placed in the bell, sort of like a large mute. Over 200 years ago, players found that putting their hand in the bell of the horn made it easier to play some notes, and the habit has never been lost. This adds to the unique sound of the horn.

EARLY HORNS

The modern horn has changed over the years. At first it was one of the simplest brass instruments. It rapidly evolved from a hollowed-out animal horn with a mouthpiece, into what was called a "helical" horn. Helical horns look like a cross between a snail and a rolled-up garden hose. The mouthpiece connects to the center of a coil of piping that curls outward to the bell. By the 17th century, the shape had become simpler. Three elegant coils of pipe formed a large loop similar in shape to the modern horn, but without all the pipe work in the middle. This simple triple-coil horn was called a *trompe*. The name, and this type of horn, comes from France, which is how the instrument became known as the French horn.

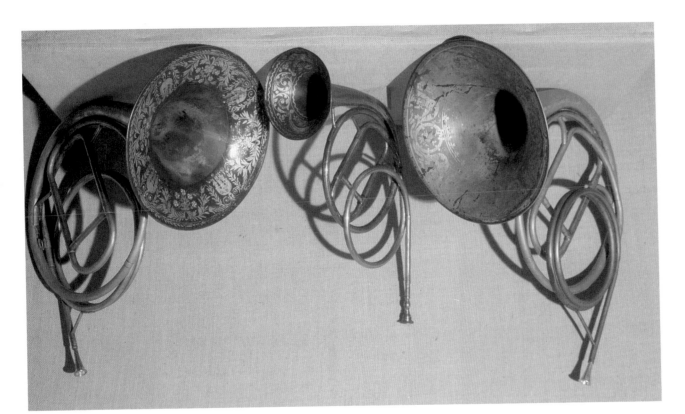

Three early 18th-century French horns

CROOKS

If a *trompe* player wanted to change key, it was necessary to change to a different instrument, because the triple-coil horn could only sound in one key. This was clumsy and difficult for players, so instrument makers tried to build a horn that could play in several keys. The earliest of these inventions was made in Vienna around 1700. The Leichnamschneider brothers made a set of rings of tube, called crooks, that could be fitted onto the horn, one by one or together, to add to its length. This allowed it to be played in any key and worked reasonably well. The player, however, had to carry around up to eight pieces of additional piping, and the instrument case began to look as if it belonged to a plumber rather than a musician!

A French inventor named Dupont designed a horn that had all the crooks built into it. The mouthpiece could be fitted into any one of eight positions, each one connected to a different set of tubing. This invention was too heavy and too cumbersome to catch on. Eventually, around 1814, the valve was invented, and the modern type of horn was made for the first time. Some early horns have just two valves, others have more. At first, composers were wary of the new instrument, and they wrote for combinations of old- and new-style horns. By 1849, when Schumann started writing chamber music for the horn, the valve horn was accepted everywhere.

A horn similar to Dupont's with all the crooks built into it and a bar for fitting the mouthpiece

An early-music group playing French horns with sets of crooks. You can see all the extra tubing that is needed in front of the player on the right.

The Modern Horn

If you look carefully at the horns in the orchestra, you'll see that their valves look different from those of the trumpets and tubas. Horns have rotary valves, and they're operated by **keys** — long elegant levers that are built in the shape of daisy petals. The valves themselves are behind the row of disks at the bottom of the levers. When the player presses the key, a small cylinder behind the disk swivels and opens up a new length of tube that changes the length of the horn's sound pipe, and alters the notes played.

Horns are generally built in the key of F. This means the parts written by composers are rather hard to play, especially where there are many high notes. To get around this problem, most horns are "double" instruments, with a second set of pipe work that instantly changes the notes that are being played to the higher pitch of B♭. If you look at the horn's keys, you'll see one tucked away under the rest of the valves, set sideways. This valve is worked by the left thumb, and it opens the pipes for the "double" horn tubing.

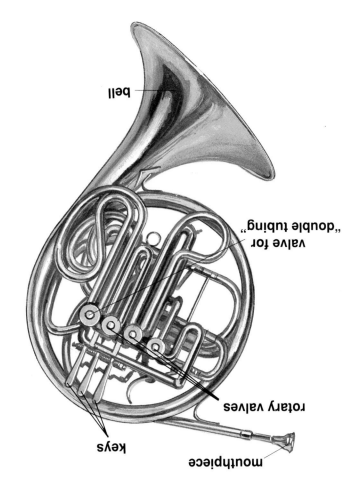

mouthpiece

keys

rotary valves

valve for "double tubing"

bell

A modern "double" French horn

24

Horn Playing

The horn is one of the more difficult brass instruments to learn to play. You need to learn how to use you right hand in the bell, while operating the keys with the left and changing the notes with your lips. Once you've mastered the basics, there is a great variety of music you can play, and the horn can be used in chamber groups, wind ensembles, and orchestras, as well as played on its own. Since most symphony orchestras need several horns, you will find that good horn players are always welcome in youth or school orchestras, and there are often vacancies!

Listening Guide

The most famous pieces for horn include the four concertos by Mozart. He wrote these for his friend Joseph Leutgeb, an amateur musician who made and sold cheese for a living. They were for the **natural horn** with no valves and would have required the greatest skill to play. Each finishes with a rousing movement based on hunting calls, reminding us that the horn was originally a hunting instrument. Mozart also wrote chamber music and his famous "Rondo" for the horn. Richard Strauss wrote horn concertos, and Brahms, Schumann, and Hindemith have all written chamber pieces for the horn. Hindemith's works include the *Concerto for Horn and Orchestra*.

Brass Band Instruments

If you go to see a brass band, you'll notice a number of instruments that look like small tubas. The E♭ horn, baritone horn, and euphonium are members of a family designed to play all the harmonies in brass band music. They support the tunes played by trumpets, cornets, and trombones. They were originally a haphazard collection of shapes and sizes, but the modern instruments were invented by Adolphe Sax around 1850. He was the same man who invented the saxophone family of woodwind instruments. In France, his brass instruments are still called "saxhorns."

All these band instruments are distantly related to the bugle. The flugelhorn is really part of this family, too, and it has tubes that resemble its width and profile. Band musicians call the family the "background brass."

In the front of the brass band below you can see the tuba-shaped instruments of the "background brass," between the full-sized tubas at each end.

E♭ HORN

This is the smallest instrument made in the shape of a tuba. It is the alto member of the family, and most brass bands have three of them. This instrument is fairly light, and it can be carried in a marching band without requiring a sling around the player's neck to help support its weight.

BARITONE HORN

This member of the background brass family is about 8 inches (20 cm) longer than the alto horn, making it 26 inches (67 cm) from end to end. At this size, it's less easy to carry than its smaller relation, and is often supported by a sling. The alto horn never appears in the symphony orchestra, but there are one or two parts for the baritone, in music by Mahler, for example.

EUPHONIUM

Only one size smaller than the tuba, the euphonium is a deep melodious instrument, and it quite often has melodies written for it in brass band pieces. Composers of orchestral music like it, too, and call it the "tenor tuba." Like all the members of the saxhorn family, the euphonium has at least three **piston valves** that work in the same way as on a trumpet.

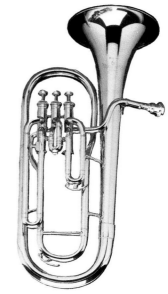

The E♭ horn

Brass Playing

To learn these instruments, you'll probably also want to play brass band music, because this is what they were invented for. Most bands encourage young players, and band music has always been written with a mixture of difficult parts (for experienced players) and easier ones for beginners. It is really an exciting experience to share in the sound of a big brass band.

In this brass band you can see two euphoniums at each end of the third row, on either side of two cornet players. The tubas in front show the difference in size.

More Brass Instruments

Few families of instruments have quite so many different varieties as the brass. Sometimes instruments that look like one member of the family turn out to be something else altogether. Two examples are the mellophone, which looks like a French horn, and the Wagner tuba, which looks like a cross between a baby helicon and a swollen French horn!

Around the world, there are lip-reed instruments that are made from all kinds of materials and are used in all sorts of ways, but which work in exactly the same way as the bugle or the simple horn does.

THE MELLOPHONE

The mellophone is the same shape and size as a French horn, but if you look closely at it you'll see that it has only one length of tube, rather than the double loop of the horn. It is more accurate than the horn in the lower part of its range, and it is sometimes used by beginners. It is used in brass bands to make a sound very similar to the French horn.

THE WAGNER TUBA

Wagner invented this strange-looking cross between a tuba and horn for the brass effects he wanted in his operas, especially his *Ring cycle*, which tells stories of the ancient Norse gods. The Wagner tuba comes in two sizes (tenor and bass), and the composer wrote for two of each. Other composers have liked this deep brassy sound, and the instrument appears in pieces by Stravinsky and Bruckner.

WORLD BRASS

The *didgeridoo* from Australia is made from a eucalyptus branch hollowed out by termites! The hollow branches, which have to be over three feet long and fairly straight, are carved slightly at each end, to shape a mouthpiece and a bell. The player makes a long droning note, and expert musicians can hum or sing other notes at the same time, creating an extraordinary effect.

The *shofar*, or ram's horn, from the Bible is used by Jewish communities around the world, and is still made from an animal horn. In the South Pacific, conch shells have a bamboo mouthpiece added to the pointed end and are turned into simple bugles. The shells are used in the same way as bugles—to give warnings at sea, to signal in battle, and to announce important events.

A bass Wagner tuba

The musician on the left of this group of Australian aborigines is playing the *didgeridoo*. The players are all in traditional costume and body paint, and some similar designs are carved and painted on the *didgeridoo* itself.

This musician, from a Hare Krishna temple, is playing a conch shell trumpet. Not only do these instruments have a distinctive sound, but the delicate coloring of the inside of the shell makes them extremely beautiful.

The *shofar* being played here in its native country, Israel, is made from a ram's horn.

Glossary

air column   length of air in the sound pipe which is made to vibrate

alto   lower range of notes sung by a female voice

baritone   medium range of notes sung by an adult male voice

bass   lowest range of notes sung by an adult male voice

bell   the widened portion of tube at the end of the instrument farthest from the player

♭ (flat)   the sign used for musical notes to show a change in the note value. The (♭) flat lowers the note value by a half step.

chord   group of notes sounded together

embouchure   the player's lips and the muscles that control them

fundamental   the lowest note of the harmonic series

harmonic series   the series of overtones or tonal shadings which can be obtained from a tube of a given length

keys   1. the levers that operate the rotary valves of a French horn
2. levers with a spring that operate a pad over the sound hole at one end and are worked by the player's finger at the other

legato   a smooth, flowing way of playing an instrument

lip reed   the vibration of the lips against a brass instrument mouthpiece, making the air in the air column vibrate

mouthpiece   the section of an instrument the player blows into and which, with the lips, forms a lip reed

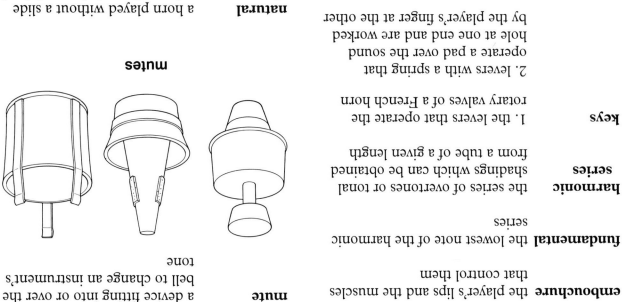

tuba mouthpiece

mutes

multi-phonics   playing several notes at the same time

mute   a device fitting into or over the bell to change an instrument's tone

natural horn   a horn played without a slide valve or finger holes, and that has only one harmonic series

octave eight notes of a complete scale

piston valve a valve that moves up and down like a sliding piston, lengthening or shortening the tubing of a brass instrument

pitch the level of a note, indicated by its position on the scale

profile cross section of an instrument

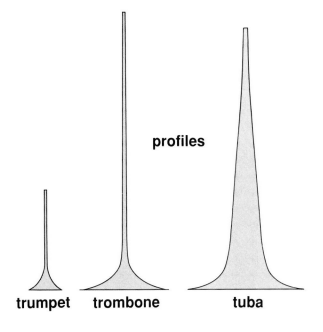

profiles

trumpet trombone tuba

rotary valve valve that turns or pivots around a central point, lengthening or shortening the tubing of a brass instrument

section a group of players of similar instruments, for example, brass section, horn section

slide U-shaped tubing that slides outside or inside two other lengths of tubing to change the pitch of an instrument

tenor highest range of notes sung by the adult male voice

tone how clear a sound is – the quality or clarity of a sound

tuning slides a slide that enables a player to tune either the whole instrument or one valve at a time

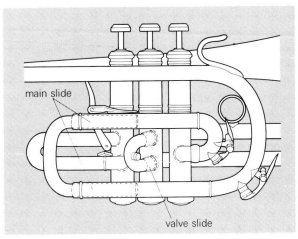

main slide

valve slide

tuning slides

valve a device that directs air into additional tubing

vibrato a trembling effect in playing an instrument

volume how loud a sound is

31

Index